Kindergarten Math Workbook

W9-CHT-804

This book belongs to:

_____

This is a kindergarten math workbook to help kids learn to count, follow directions, learn patterns, practice addition & subtraction, learn about time and money and many more math concepts in a fun and engaging way.

This book is organized in a progressively skill building way for kids to develop confidence and a love for math.

This book requires guidance from a parent, teacher or care giver to help the child follow the worksheets.

Practice Number Addition, Subtraction, Measurement, Shapes, Time and Money

This Kindergarten Math workbook is divided into the following parts:

Part 1

After, Before & Between
Less & More
Make 10 & 20
Skip Counting by 2s, 5s, 10s

Part 2

Shapes:
2D Shapes
Shape Patterns
3D Shapes

Part 3

Measurement:
Light & Heavy
Long & Short
More & Less
Tall & Short
Wide & Narrow
Positions:
Left, Middle & Right
Top, Middle & Bottom
Above & Below
Inside & Outside
Probability:
More or Less Likely

Part 4

Learning Addition:
Finger Addition
Number Lines
Dice Addition
Fill in the missing number
Match the objects
Number Bonds
Word Problems

Part 5

Learning Subtraction:
Finger Subtraction
Number Lines
Fill in the missing number
Match the objects
Word Problems

Part 6

Time:
Analog Clock
Read the Clock & Tell Time
Digital Clock
Match Analog & Digital Clocks

Part 7

Money:
Coin Names
Coin Values
Count Money

Hi Parents,

Congrats on choosing "Kindergarten Math" for your kiddo's math journey! Your kid's math skills are about to soar!

We've got a surprise for you! We're giving away a complimentary **FREE 50-page Kindergarten Math eBook** to supercharge your kid's math learning experience! That's right, you get a whole extra book for **FREE!**

To get this ebook, email me at

sujatha.lalgudi@gmail.com

Title the email **"KG Math"** to get your copy of the free Math eBook!

Thank you
Sujatha Lalgudi

Meet Jojo.
Jojo is a curious elephant.
He loves to learn and play.
Learn to do math along with Jojo!

Are you ready?
Let's go!

Part 1:

After, Before, In Between

Practice number sequence upto 20.

Less & More

Count the objects to find out which is less/more.
Color the objects.

Make 10, 20

Count the circles and draw more to make 10, 20.

Skip-Count

Skip count by 2s, 5s & 10s.

You are AWESOME!

AFTER
Write the number that comes **after** these numbers

7	8	_9_
10	11	_12_
4	5	___
12	13	___
8	9	___
17	18	___
6	7	___
18	19	___
5	6	___
14	15	___
3	4	___
16	17	___

AFTER
Write the number that comes **after** these numbers

2 3 ____	8 9 ____
11 12 ____	6 7 ____
9 10 ____	4 5 ____
13 14 ____	16 17 ____
1 2 ____	10 11 ____
15 16 ____	17 18 ____

BEFORE
Write the number that comes **before** these numbers

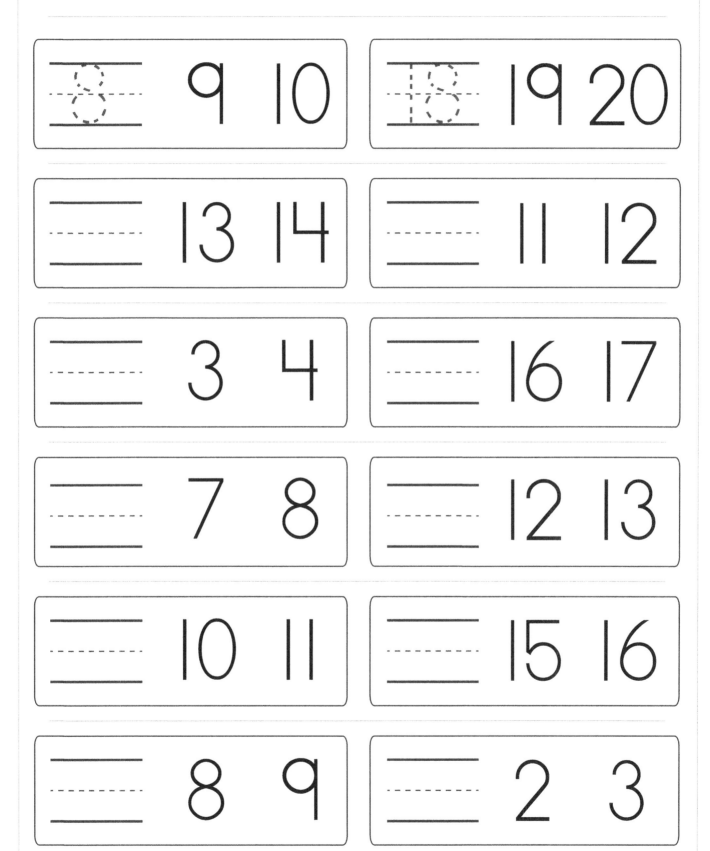

BEFORE
Write the number that comes **before** these numbers

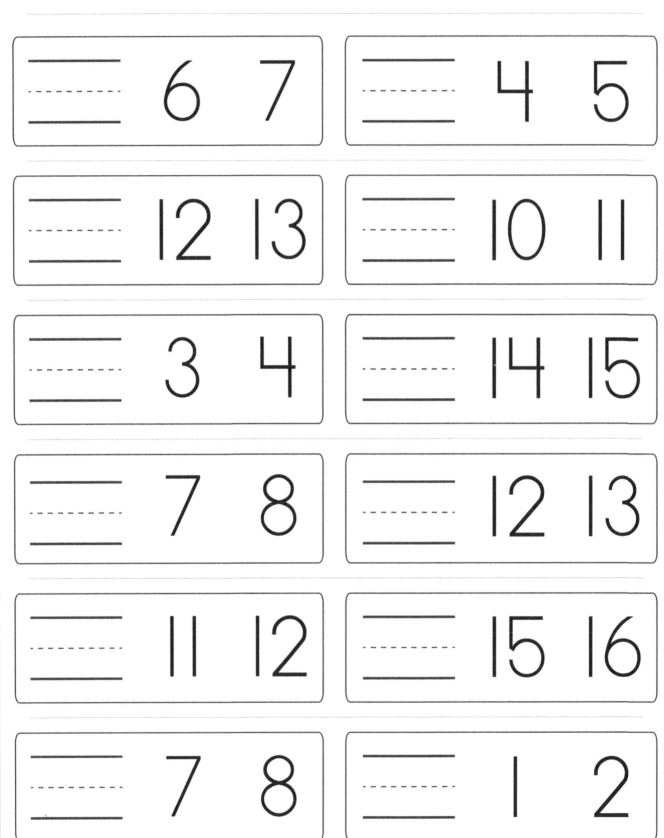

6 7

4 5

12 13

10 11

3 4

14 15

7 8

12 13

11 12

15 16

7 8

1 2

IN BETWEEN
Write the number that comes **in between** these numbers

9 10 11	6 7 8
10 ___ 12	18 ___ 20
7 ___ 9	15 ___ 17
0 ___ 2	11 ___ 13
17 ___ 19	16 ___ 18
8 ___ 10	2 ___ 4

IN BETWEEN
Write the number that comes **in between** these numbers

5 _____ 7	7 _____ 9
15 _____ 17	11 _____ 13
9 _____ 11	14 _____ 16
1 _____ 3	13 _____ 15
12 _____ 14	17 _____ 19
3 _____ 5	4 _____ 6

LESS

Count the unicorns in each group. Color the group that has less.
Complete the number sentence.

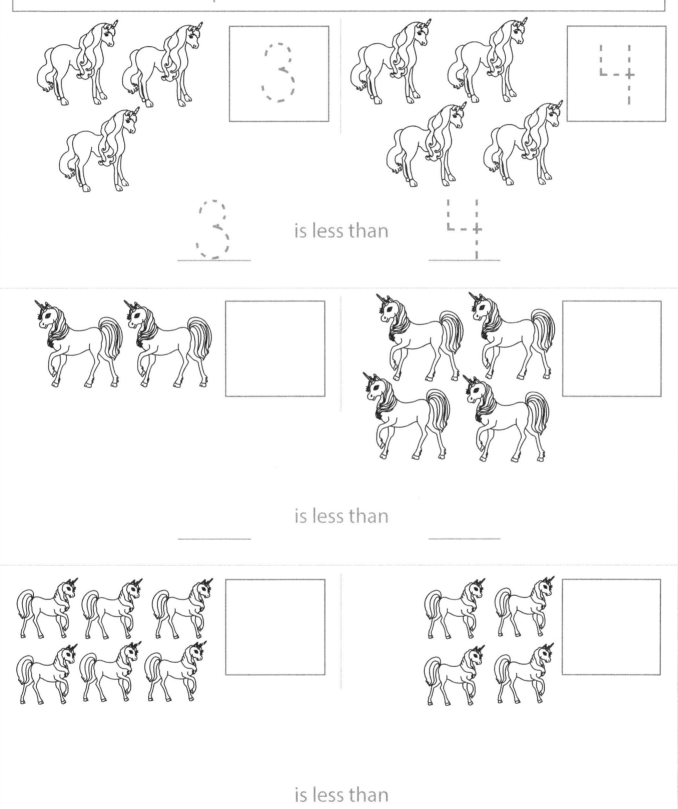

3   is less than   4

_____ is less than _____

_____ is less than _____

LESS

Count the cupcakes in each group. Color the group that has less.
Complete the number sentence.

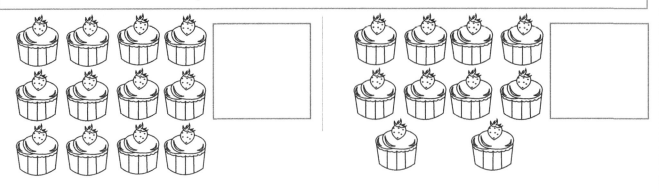

is less than

_____   _____

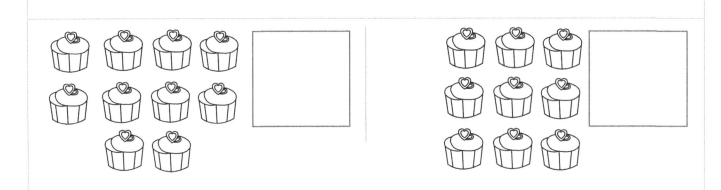

is less than

_____   _____

is less than

_____   _____

MORE

Count the fish in each group. Color the group that has more.
Complete the number sentence.

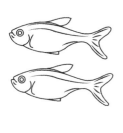  2     4

4 is more than 2

 [ ]   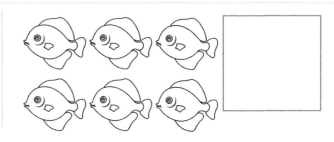 [ ]

is more than

_____   _____

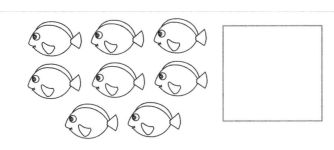  [ ]   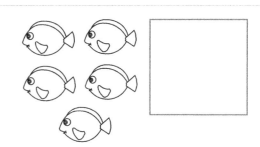 [ ]

is more than

_____   _____

13

MORE

Count the jets in each group. Color the group that has more.
Complete the number sentence.

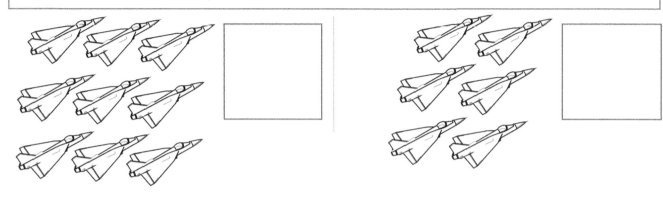

is more than

_____   _____

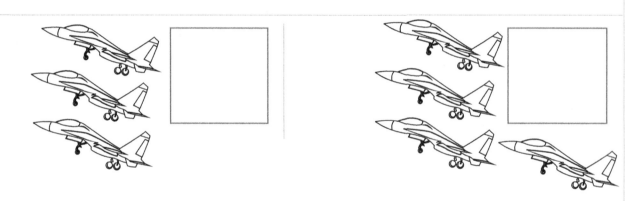

is more than

_____   _____

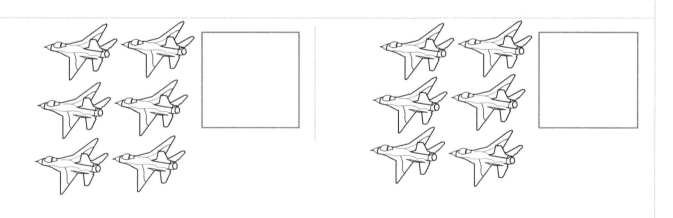

is more than

_____   _____

MAKE 10

Draw more to make 10.
Complete the number sentence.

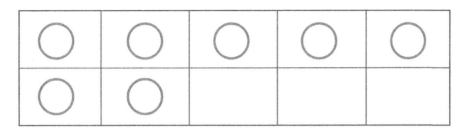

$$7 \; + \; 3 \; = \; 10$$

$$\underline{\hspace{1.5cm}} \; + \; \underline{\hspace{1.5cm}} \; = \; \boxed{}$$

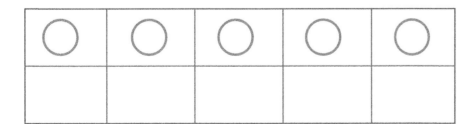

$$\underline{\hspace{1.5cm}} \; + \; \underline{\hspace{1.5cm}} \; = \; \boxed{}$$

MAKE 10

Draw more to make 10.
Complete the number sentence.

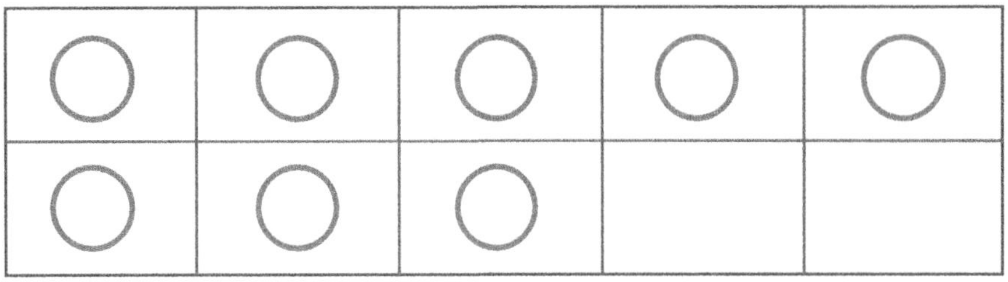

_____   **+**   _____   **=**

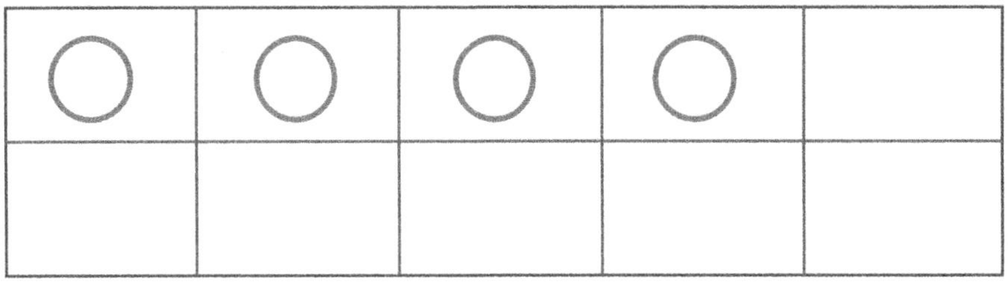

_____   **+**   _____   **=**

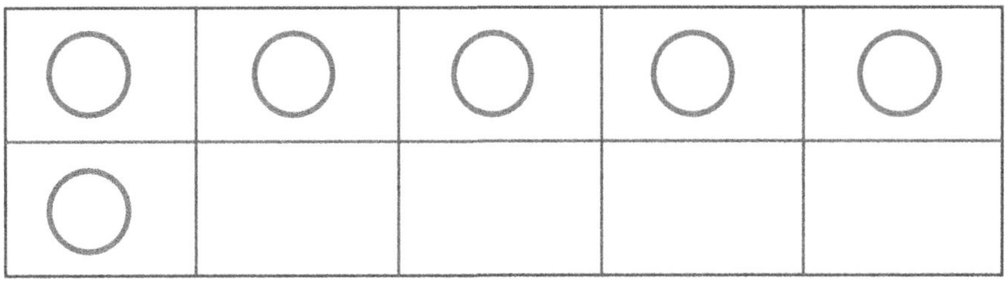

_____   **+**   _____   **=**

MAKE 20

Draw more to make 20.
Complete the number sentence.

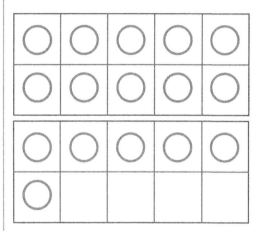 + =

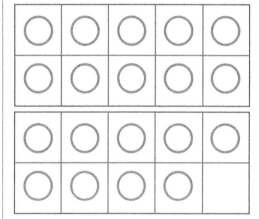 + ____ =

____ + ____ =

MAKE 20

Draw more to make 20.
Complete the number sentence.

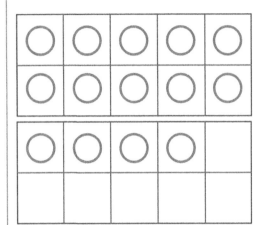 _____

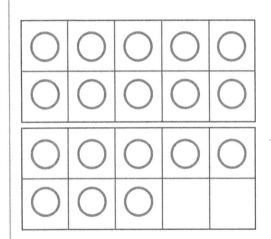 _____ + _____ =

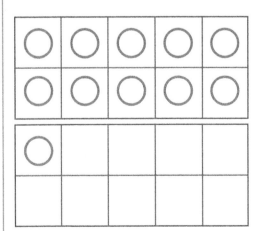 _____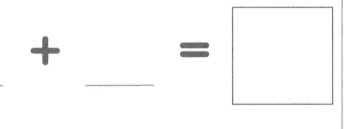

COUNT BY 2s

Write in each missing number to count by 2s.
Color the page.

2			8		12
	16			22	
		30			
38			44		
				58	
		66			

74						86
		92				100

COUNT BY 5s

Write in each missing number to count by 5s.
Color the hands.

COUNT BY 10s

Write in each missing number to count by 10s.
Color the stars.

Part 2:

2D Shapes

Learn to identify the 2D shapes.
Match the shapes to everyday objects.

Patterns

Complete shape patterns.

3D Shapes

Learn to identify the 3D shapes.
Match the shapes to everyday objects.

You are
AMAZING!

2D SHAPES
Trace the shapes and learn about them.
Color the shapes.

CIRCLE

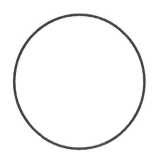   

A circle is a shape that is round. It has no corners and no sides.

OVAL

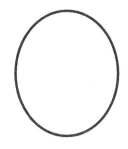   

An oval is a shape that is almost round. It has no corners and no sides.

TRIANGLE

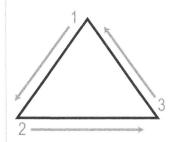 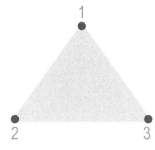 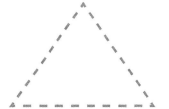 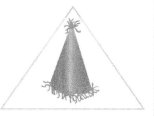

A triangle has **3** sides and **3** corners. It is not round.

2D SHAPES
Learn about the shapes and trace them.
Color the shapes.

SQUARE

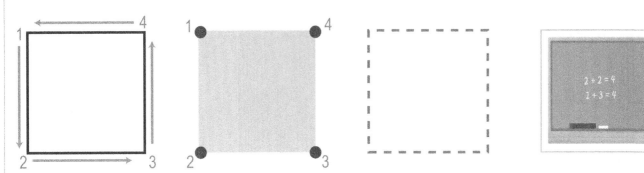

A Square has **4** equal sides and **4** corners.

RECTANGLE

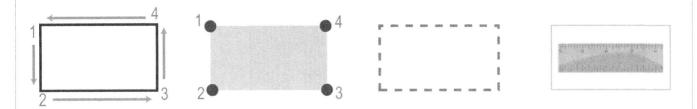

A Rectangle has **4** sides. **2** sides are longer than the opposite sides.

HEXAGON

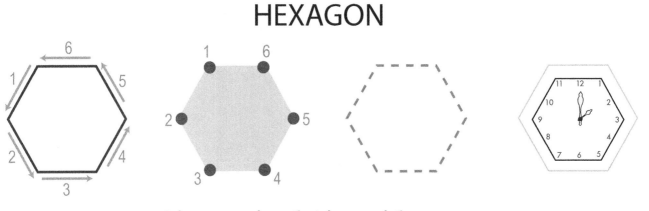

A hexagon has **6** sides and **6** corners.

2D SHAPES

Match the shapes to the objects.
Color them.

2D SHAPES

Name each shape. Count the sides of each shape.
Circle the correct answer.

Rectangle: 3 5 (4)	Circle: 1 0 2
Triangle: 3 1 5	Square: 2 3 4
Hexagon: 7 8 6	Oval: 2 1 0

PATTERNS
Draw the shape that comes next in the pattern

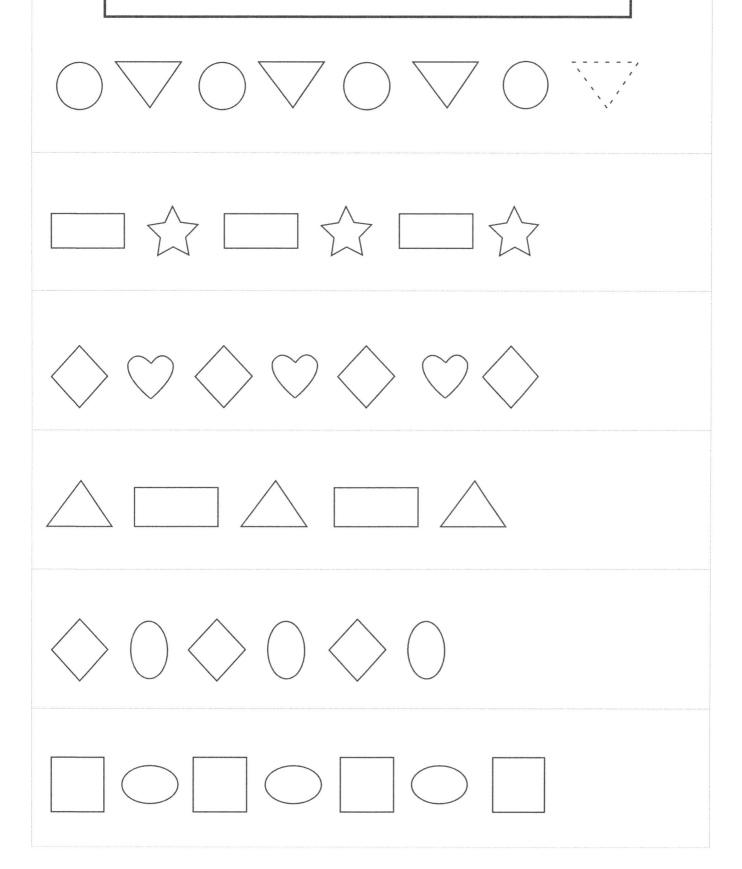

PATTERNS
Draw the shape that comes next in the pattern

3D Shape - CUBE
A Cube has 6 flat surfaces. They are all squares.
Count each colored square.

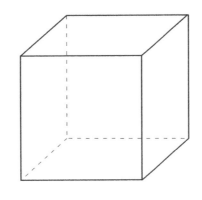

CUBE

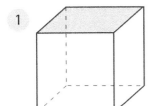 1

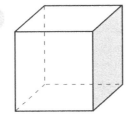 2

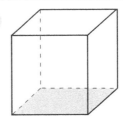 3

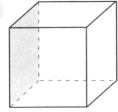 4

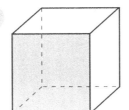 5

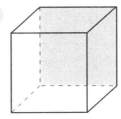 6

Example of an everyday object shaped like a cube:

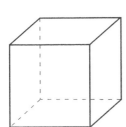

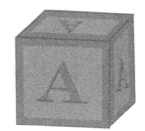

Alphabet Block

3D Shape - CYLINDER
A Cylinder has 2 flat surfaces.
The 2 flat surfaces are circles. The rest of the cylinder is curved.

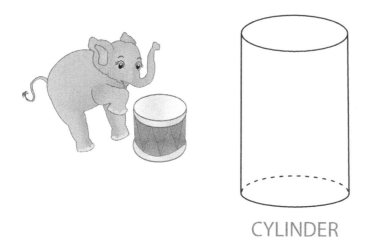

CYLINDER

Circle

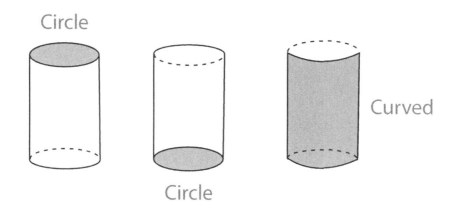

Circle

Curved

Example of an everyday object shaped like a cylinder:

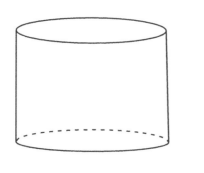

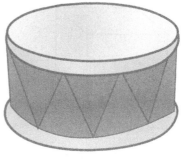

Drum

3D Shape - CONE
A Cone is curved. It has a pointy tip.
The flat surface on a cone is a circle.

CONE

Tip

Curved

Flat

Example of an everyday object shaped like a cone:

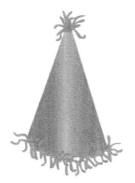

Party Hat

3D Shape - SPHERE

A Sphere is a round shape. It has no flat surfaces or corners.

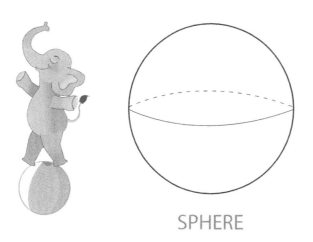

SPHERE

Which shape is a sphere?
Put a check (✔) in the box with the correct answer.

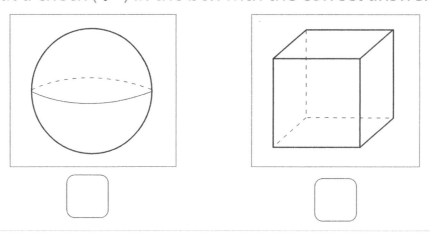

Example of an everyday object shaped like a sphere:

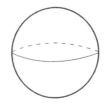 

Football

Identify the 3D Shapes

Put a check (✔) in the box with the correct answer.

Which shape is a Cone?

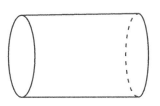
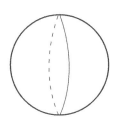

Which shape is a Cube?

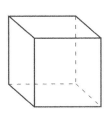
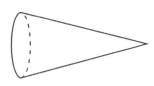
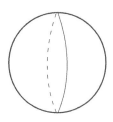

Which shape is a Cylinder?

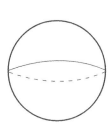
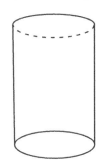
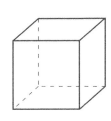

Identify the 3D Shapes

Put a check (✔) in the box with the correct answer.

Which shape is a Sphere?

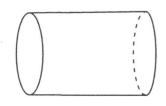

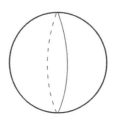

Which shape is a Cylinder?

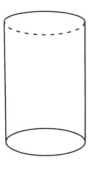

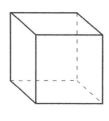

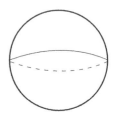

Which shape is a Cone?

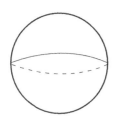

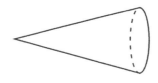

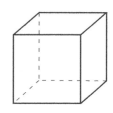

Part 3:

Measurement

Light & Heavy
Long & Short
More & Less
Tall & Short
Wide & Narrow

Positions

Left, Middle & Right
Top, Middle & Bottom
Above & Below
Inside & Outside

Prabability

More or Less Likely

Great Going!

LIGHT	HEAVY
LIGHT Which one is lighter? Put a check (✔) in the box with the correct answer	**HEAVY** Which one is heavier? Put a check (✔) in the box with the correct answer

✔   ☐   ✔   ☐

☐   ☐   ☐   ☐

☐   ☐   ☐   ☐

LONG	SHORT
Which one is longer? Put a check (✔) in the box with the correct answer	Which one is shorter? Put a check (✔) in the box with the correct answer

 ✔

  ✔

 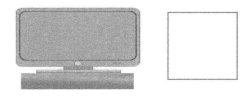

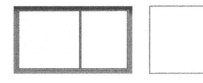 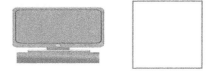

 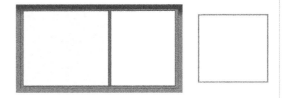

MORE	LESS
MORE Which one holds more? Put a check (✔) in the box with the correct answer	**LESS** Which one holds less? Put a check (✔) in the box with the correct answer

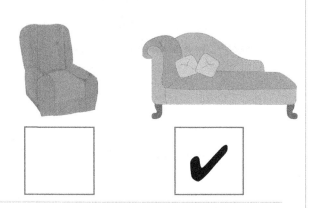

☐   ✔

☐   ✔

☐   ☐

☐   ☐

☐   ☐

☐   ☐

TALL
Which one is taller?
Put a check (✔) in the box
with the correct answer

SHORT
Which one is shorter?
Put a check (✔) in the box
with the correct answer

 ✔ ✔

WIDE	NARROW
WIDE Which one is wider? Put a check (✔) in the box with the correct answer	**NARROW** Which one is narrower? Put a check (✔) in the box with the correct answer

☐ ✔

☐ ✔

☐ ☐ ☐ ☐

☐ ☐ ☐ ☐

Practice recognizing Left, Middle & Right

 LEFT  MIDDLE RIGHT

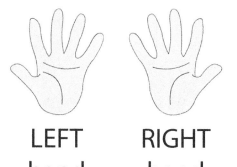

LEFT hand   RIGHT hand

Practice recognizing left & right by looking at your palms

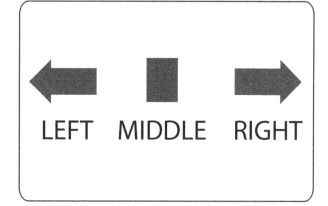

LEFT   MIDDLE   RIGHT

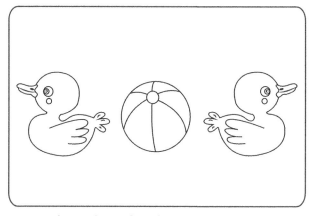

Color the duck on the right

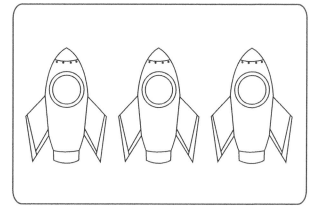

Color the rocket on the left

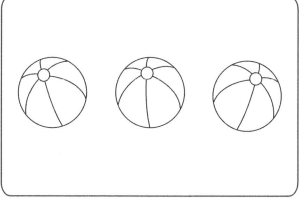

Color the ball inthe middle

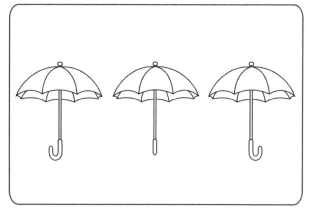

Color the umbrella on the right

Answer the questions by recognizing Left, Middle & Right.

Color the balloon in the middle

Color the cat on the right

Color the fox on the left

Color the carrot in the middle

Color the bow on the right

Color the fish in the middle

TOP, MIDDLE, BOTTOM

Look at the object in each box.
Learn to recognize where each of them is placed.

Color the ball at the bottom

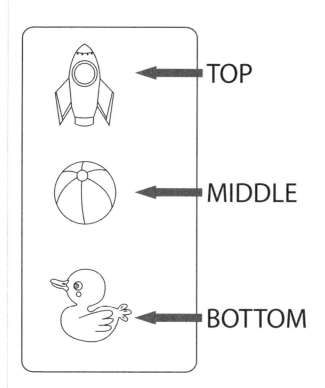

TOP

MIDDLE

BOTTOM

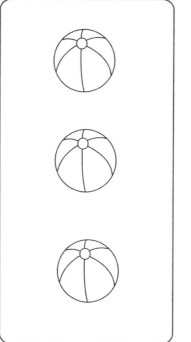

Color the duck at the middle

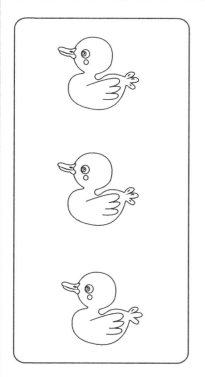

Color the rocket at the top

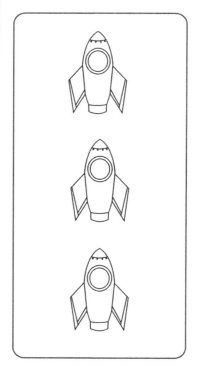

TOP, MIDDLE, BOTTOM

Look at the object in each box.
Learn to recognize where each of them is placed.

Color the umbrella at the top

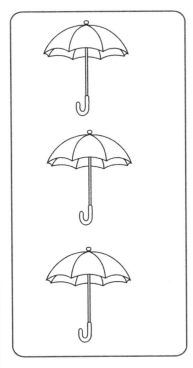

Color the rocket in the middle

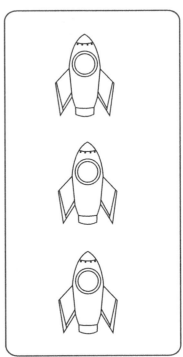

Color the ball at the bottom

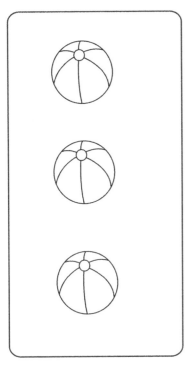

Color the duck at the top

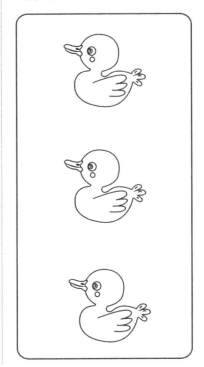

POSITIONS
ABOVE & BELOW
Put a check (✔) in the box with the correct answer.

ABOVE

BELOW

Which object is Below?

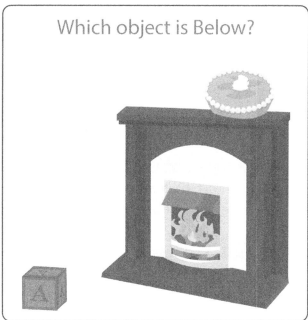

☐    ☐

Which object is Above?

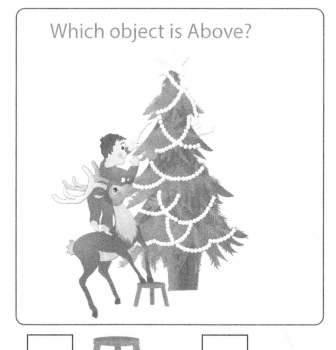

☐   ☐ ✦

Which object is Below?

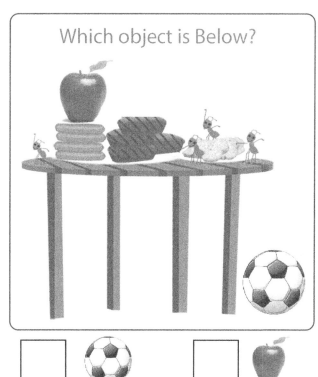

☐   ☐

POSITIONS
INSIDE & OUTSIDE
Put a check (✔) in the box with the correct answer.

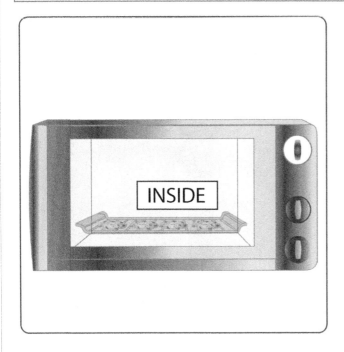

Which picture shows the cow standing outside the barn?

PROBABILITY

Look at the spinner. On which color is the spinner likely to land?
Put a check (✔) in the box with the correct answer.

Observe which part is larger.
More of the circle is white than gray.
The spinner is more likely to land on white.

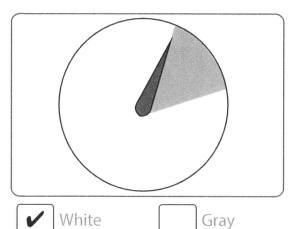

✔ White   ☐ Gray

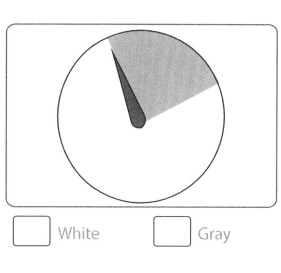

☐ White   ☐ Gray

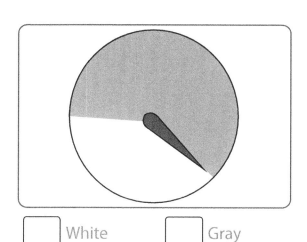

☐ White   ☐ Gray

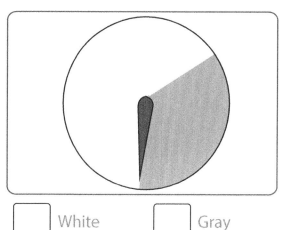

☐ White   ☐ Gray

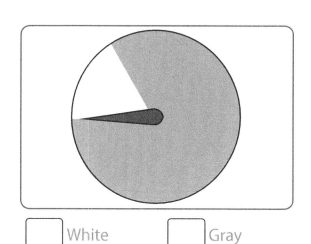

☐ White   ☐ Gray

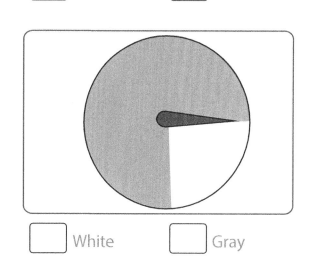

☐ White   ☐ Gray

PROBABILITY
How likely are you to pick up the shape?
Put a check (✔) in the box with the correct answer.

| ☐ More Likely | ✔ Less Likely |

| ☐ More Likely | ☐ Less Likely |

| ☐ More Likely | ☐ Less Likely |

| ☐ More Likely | ☐ Less Likely |

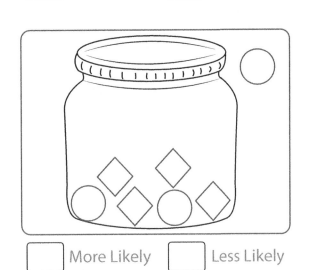

| ☐ More Likely | ☐ Less Likely |

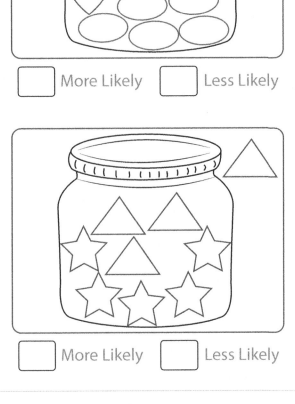

| ☐ More Likely | ☐ Less Likely |

Part 4:

Learning Addition

Finger Addition
Number Lines
Dice Addition
Fill in the missing number
Match the objects
Number Bonds
Word Problems

*Note: The addition problems using fingers are sequential to help kids identify the answer pattern. This is also designed to give them confidence to understand addition.

ADDITION

Count and add with the help of your fingers.
Write the correct numbers in the box.

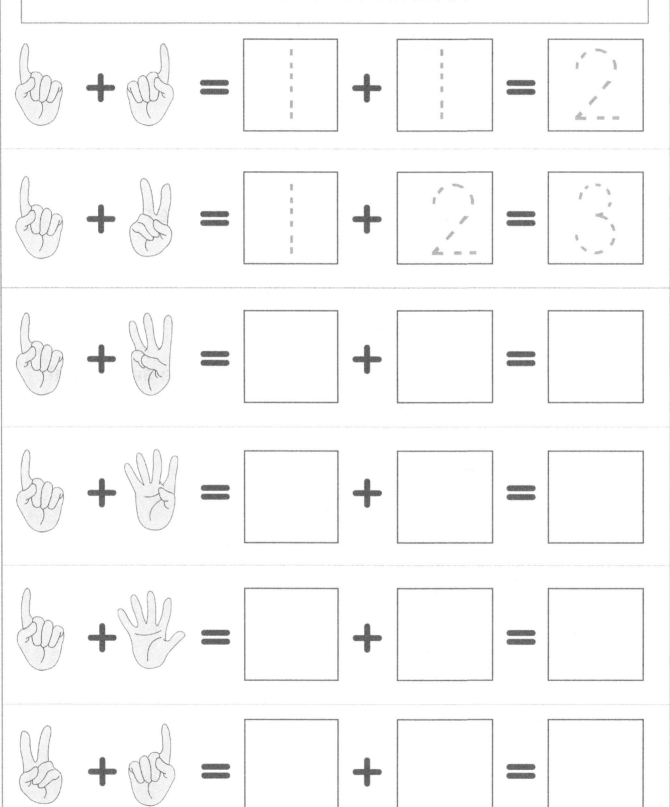

ADDITION

Count and add with the help of your fingers.
Write the correct numbers in the box.

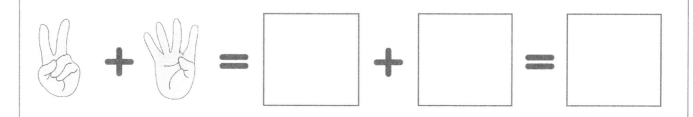

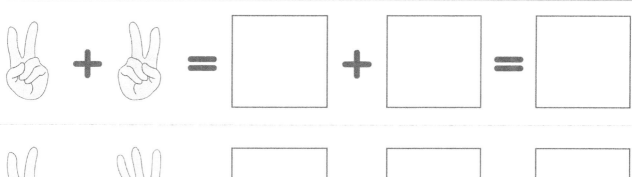

ADDITION

Count and add with the help of your fingers.
Write the correct numbers in the box.

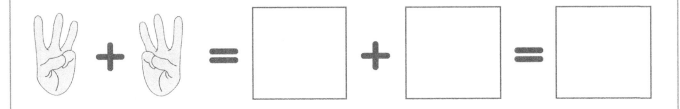

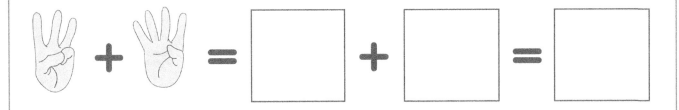

ADDITION

Count and add with the help of your fingers.
Write the correct numbers in the box.

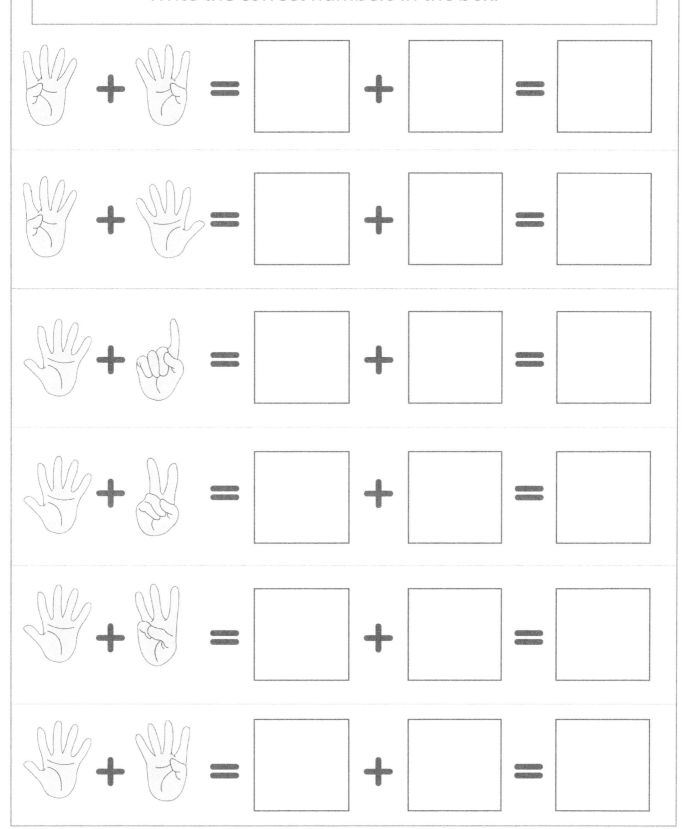

ADDITION

Count and add with the help of your fingers.
Write the correct numbers in the box.

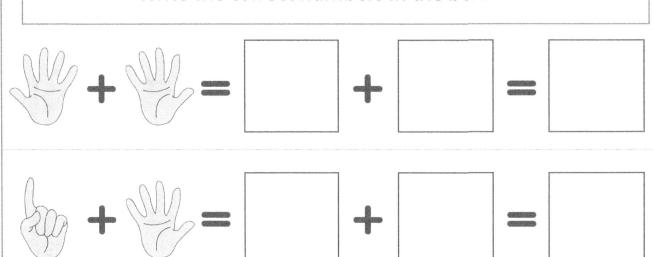

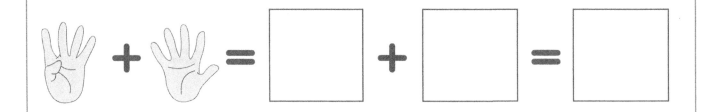

NUMBER LINES

Use the number lines to complete
the addition problems

$1 + 2 =$ 3

$5 + 3 =$ 8

$6 + 4 =$

$3 + 2 =$

$4 + 1 =$

NUMBER LINES

Use the number lines to complete
the addition problems

$2 + 3 =$ ☐ ← 0 1 2 3 4 5 6 7 8 9 10 →

$5 + 1 =$ ☐ ← 0 1 2 3 4 5 6 7 8 9 10 →

$7 + 3 =$ ☐ ← 0 1 2 3 4 5 6 7 8 9 10 →

$5 + 5 =$ ☐ ← 0 1 2 3 4 5 6 7 8 9 10 →

$8 + 1 =$ ☐ ← 0 1 2 3 4 5 6 7 8 9 10 →

ADDITION

Count the dots on each dice.
Add the dots and write the correct number in the box.

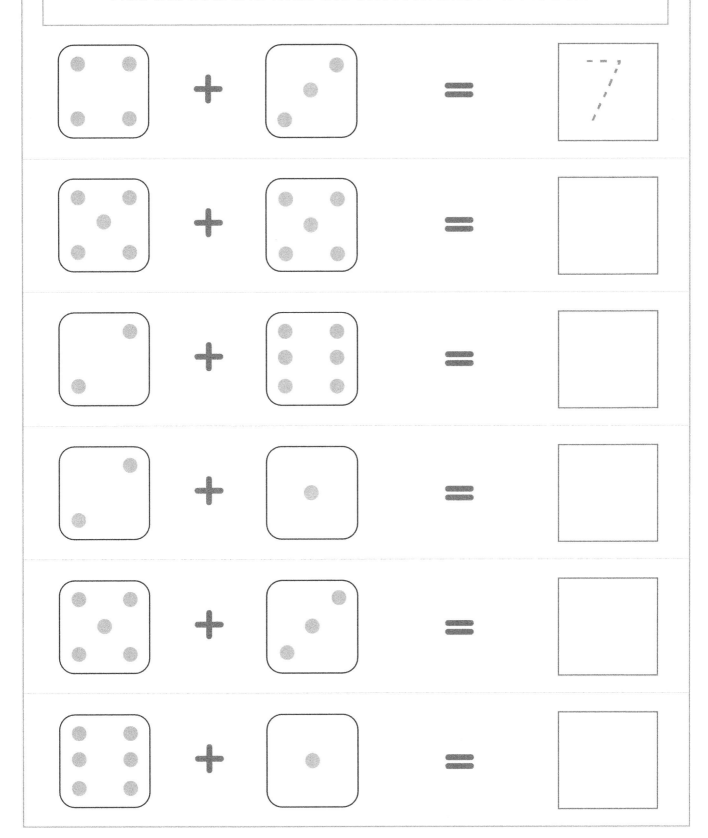

ADDITION

Count the dots on each dice.
Add the dots and write the correct number in the box.

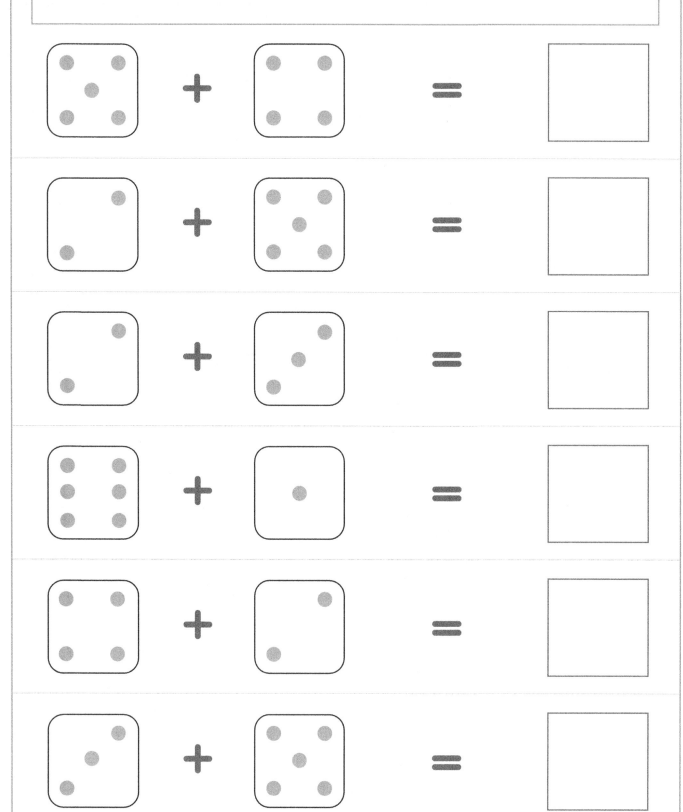

ADDITION

Fill in the missing number.

3 +  =

2 + =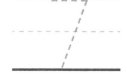

5 + =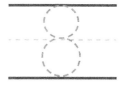

1 + =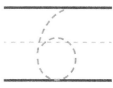

ADDITION
Fill in the missing number.

8 +  =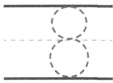

4 +  =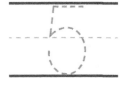

9 +  =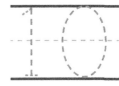

7 +  =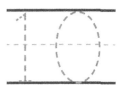

ADDITION

Draw a line to match the problem on the left with the correct number of images on the right

1 + 3 =

3 + 4 =

5 + 3 =

4 + 2 =

4 + 5 =

ADDITION

Draw a line to match the problem on the left with the correct number of images on the right

$2 + 2 =$

$4 + 2 =$

$3 + 2 =$

$5 + 2 =$

$4 + 4 =$

NUMBER BONDS

Count the dots on each domino and write down the number.
Add the numbers.

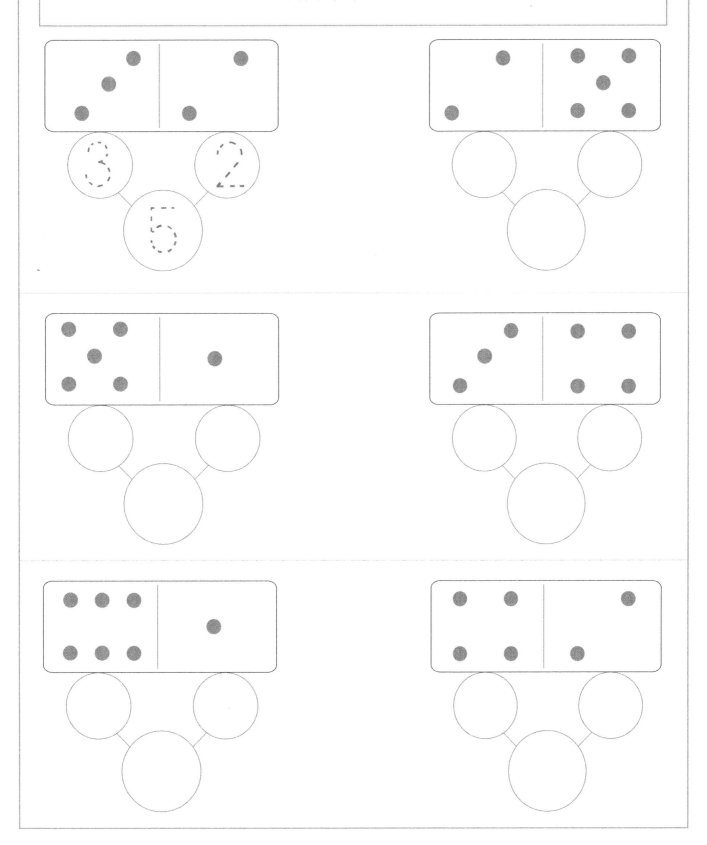

NUMBER BONDS

Count the dots on each domino and write down the number.
Add the numbers.

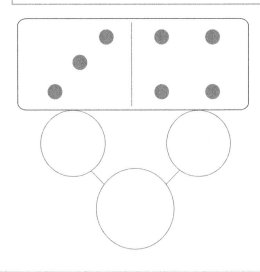

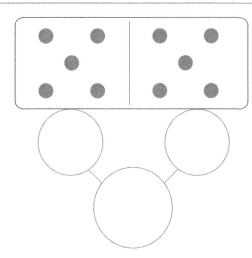

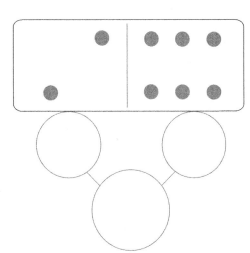

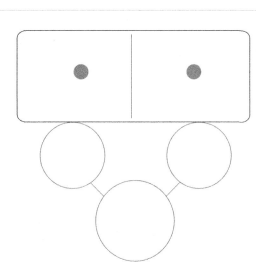

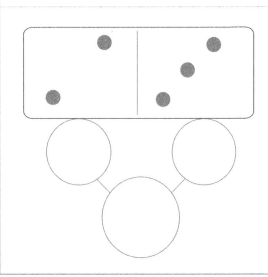

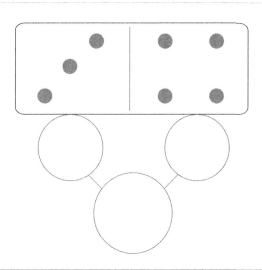

NUMBER BONDS

Count the dots on each domino and write down the number.
Add the numbers.

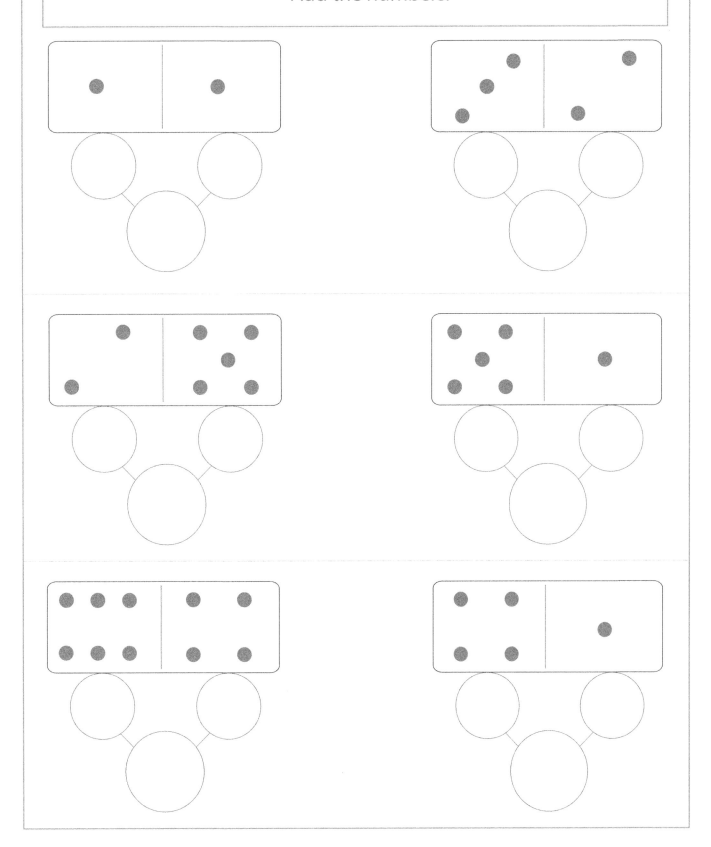

WORD PROBLEMS
Read, Color and Answer

Color 3 fish yellow and 5 fish orange.
How many fish are there in all?

Color 2 apples red and 7 apples green.
How many apples are there in all?

WORD PROBLEMS
Read, Color and Answer

Color 1 shell blue and 6 shells purple.
How many shells are there in all?

Color 4 stars orange and 6 stars yellow.
How many stars are there in all?

Part 5:

Learning Subtraction

Finger Subtraction
Number Lines
Fill in the missing number
Match the objects
Word Problems

*Note: The subtraction problems using fingers are sequential to help kids identify the answer pattern. This is also designed to give them confidence to understand subtraction.

SUBTRACTION

Subtract the number with the help of your fingers.
Write the correct numbers in the box.

 − 1 =

 − 1 =

 − 2 =

 − 1 =

 − 2 =

SUBTRACTION

Subtract the number with the help of your fingers.
Write the correct numbers in the box.

 $-$ 3 $=$

 $-$ 1 $=$

 $-$ 2 $=$

 $-$ 3 $=$

 $-$ 4 $=$

SUBTRACTION

Subtract the number with the help of your fingers.
Write the correct numbers in the box.

   −   =

   −   2   =

   −   3   = 

   −   4   = 

   −   5   = 

SUBTRACTION

Subtract the number with the help of your fingers.
Write the correct numbers in the box.

  − =

  − 2 =

  − 3 =

  − 4 =

  − 5 =

SUBTRACTION

Subtract the number with the help of your fingers.
Write the correct numbers in the box.

  − 1 = [ ]

  − 2 = [ ]

  − 3 = [ ]

  − 4 = [ ]

  − 5 = [ ]

SUBTRACTION

Subtract the number with the help of your fingers.
Write the correct numbers in the box.

 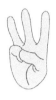 − =

  − 2 =

  − 3 =

  − 4 =

  − 5 =

SUBTRACTION

Subtract the number with the help of your fingers.
Write the correct numbers in the box.

  − =

  − 2 =

  − 3 =

  − 4 =

  − 5 =

SUBTRACTION

Subtract the number with the help of your fingers.
Write the correct numbers in the box.

  $-$ $=$

  $-$ 2 $=$

  $-$ 3 $=$

  $-$ 4 $=$

  $-$ 5 $=$

NUMBER LINES
Use the number lines to complete
the subtraction problems.

5 - 3 = [2]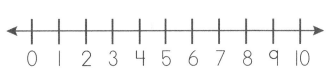

8 - 4 = [4]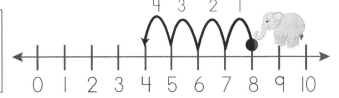

9 - 8 = [ ]

10 - 4 = [ ]

7 - 3 = [ ]

NUMBER LINES

Use the number lines to complete
the subtraction problems.

$2 - 2 = $ ☐

0 1 2 3 4 5 6 7 8 9 10

$7 - 5 = $ ☐

0 1 2 3 4 5 6 7 8 9 10

$2 - 0 = $ ☐

0 1 2 3 4 5 6 7 8 9 10

$8 - 3 = $ ☐

0 1 2 3 4 5 6 7 8 9 10

$5 - 4 = $ ☐

0 1 2 3 4 5 6 7 8 9 10

SUBTRACTION

Draw a line to match the problem on the left with the correct number of oranges on the right.

8 - 1 =

5 - 3 =

7 - 4

9 - 5 =

8 - 2 =

SUBTRACTION

Draw a line to match the problem on the left with the correct number of pineapples on the right.

$8 - 5 =$

$7 - 2 =$

$5 - 3 =$

$6 - 5 =$

$9 - 5 =$

WORD PROBLEMS
Read, Color and Answer

9 frogs are sitting on a lilly pad. 5 frogs jump into the water.
How many frogs are on the lilly pad now?

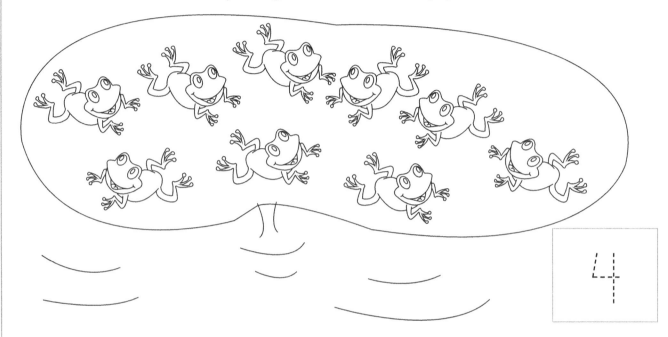

4

There are 6 apples on a tree. 3 apples fall down.
How many apples are left in the tree?

WORD PROBLEMS
Read, Color and Answer

7 crabs are on the beach.
3 crabs hide in the sand. How many crabs do you see now ?

8 bees are near the bee hive.
5 bees fly away. How many bees are left?

Part 6:

Time

Analog Clock

Read the Clock & Tell the Time

Digital Clock

Match Analog & Digital Clocks

You are
SENSATIONAL!

TELLING TIME

A clock has two hands. The short hand shows the hour. The long hand shows the minutes. When the long hand points to 12, we say o'clock.

Read and trace the time on the digital clocks.

Analog Clock:

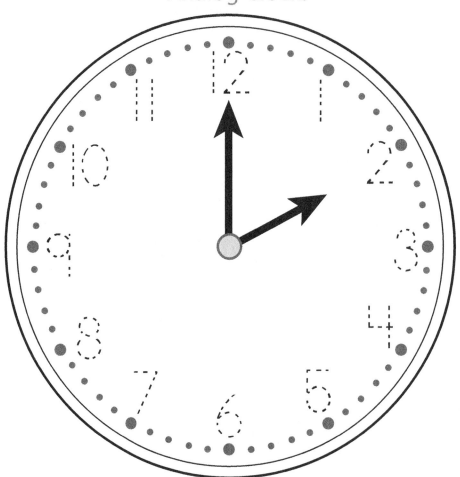

Digital Clock:

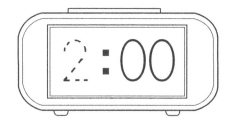

The time is 2 o'clock.

TIME
Read the clock and tell the time.
Write down the time in the box.

6 O'Clock

O'Clock

O'Clock

O'Clock

TIME
Read the clock and tell the time.
Write down the time in the box.

O'Clock

O'Clock

O'Clock

O'Clock

TIME

Read the clock and tell the time.
Write down the time in the box.

O'Clock

O'Clock

O'Clock

O'Clock

TIME
Read and trace the time on the digital clocks.
Put a check (✔) in the box with the correct answer

Which clock shows 6 O'Clock?

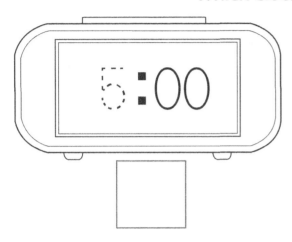 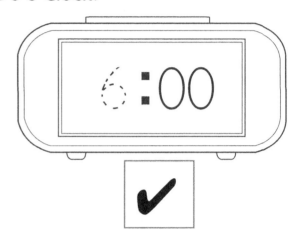

Which clock shows 2 O'Clock?

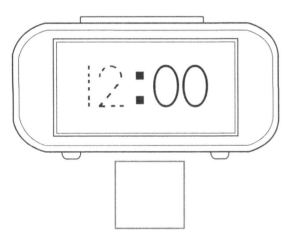 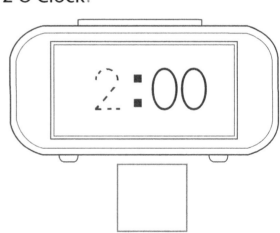

Which clock shows 9 O'Clock?

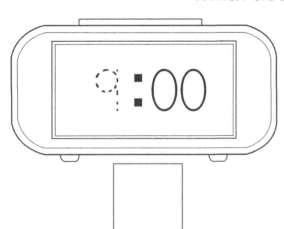 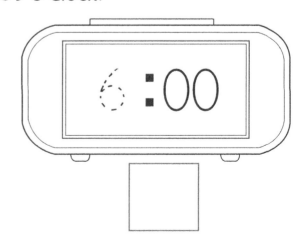

TIME

Read and trace the time on the digital clocks.
Put a check (✔) in the box with the correct answer

Which clock shows **1 O'Clock**?

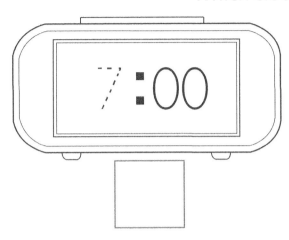 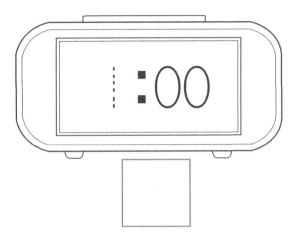

Which clock shows **8 O'Clock**?

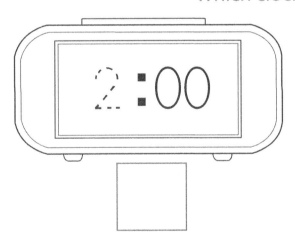 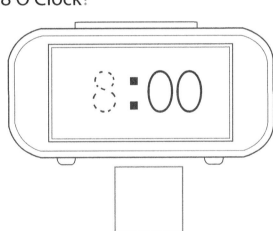

Which clock shows **3 O'Clock**?

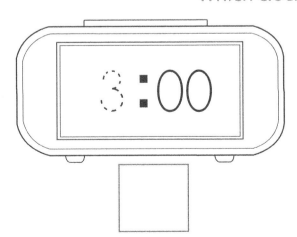 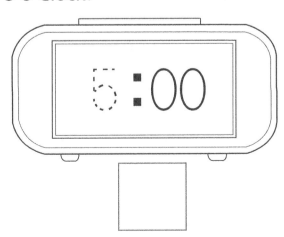

TIME

Read and trace the time on the digital clock.
Draw the small hand on the clock to show the same time.

TIME

Read and trace the time on the digital clock.
Draw the small hand on the clock to show the same time.

TIME

Read and trace the time on the digital clock.
Draw the small hand on the clock to show the same time.

TIME

Read the time on the analog clock.
Put a check (✔) in the box with the digital clock showing same time.

Part 7:

Money

Coin Names
Coin Values
Count Money

*Note: Please note that the coins in this set are not scaled to size intentionally, to provide a simplified learning experience for kids.

MONEY

Learn to recognize each coin and its value.
Color the coins and read their names out loud.

penny
1 cent

nickel
5 cents

dime
10 cents

quarter
25 cents

MONEY

Draw a line to match each coin with the correct name.
Color the coins and read the name out loud.

quarter

penny

dime

nickel

MONEY

Draw a line to match each coin with the correct amount.
Color the coins and read the amount out loud.

This is the symbol for cent:

25 cents

5 cents

1 cent

10 cents

PENNY
Fill in the correct answers.

Write the correct amount:

A **penny** is

cent.

Add up the pennies and write the amount in the box:

   ¢

   ¢

    ¢

     ¢

NICKEL

Fill in the correct answers.

Write the correct amount:

A **nickel** is

cents.

Add up the nickels and write the amount in the box:

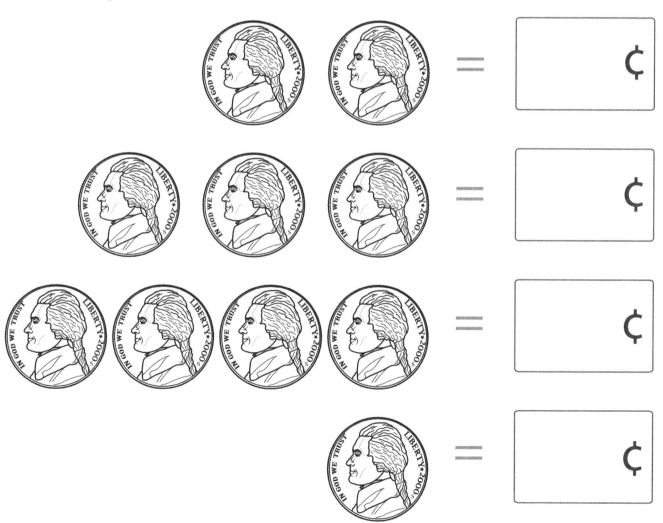

DIME
Fill in the correct answers.

Write the correct amount:

A **dime** is

 cents.

Add up the dimes and write the amount in the box:

   =  ¢

 =  ¢

  =  ¢

    =  ¢

QUARTER
Fill in the correct answers.

Write the correct amount:

A **quarter** is

cents.

Add up the quarters and write the amount in the box:

  = ¢

     = ¢

   = ¢

    = ¢

TASTY TREATS

Use the correct coin to pay for each treat.
Put a check (✔) in the box with the correct answer.

MONEY

How much money is there? Count the coins.
Put a check (✔) in the box with the correct answer.

7¢	8¢
☐	☐

20¢	30¢
☐	☐

28¢	35¢
☐	☐

40¢	30¢
☐	☐

MONEY

How much money is there? Count the coins.
Put a check (✔) in the box with the correct answer.

12¢	15¢
☐	☐

22¢	21¢
☐	☐

63¢	36¢
☐	☐

40¢	41¢
☐	☐

MONEY

Count the coins. Write the price of each fruit.
Color the fruits.

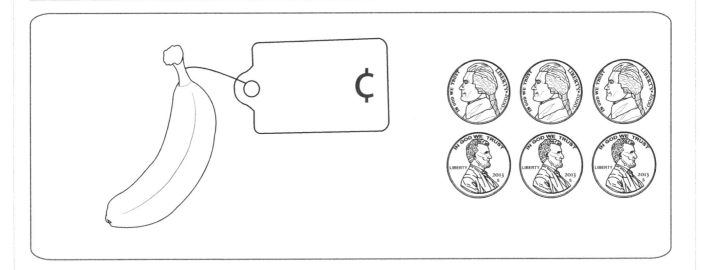

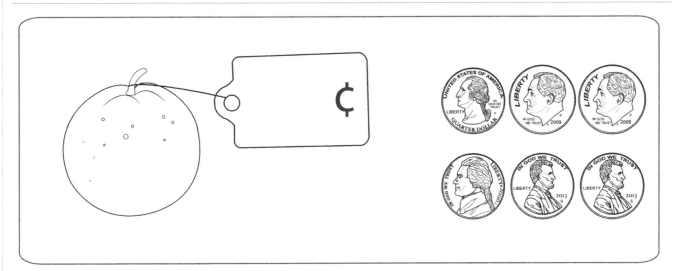

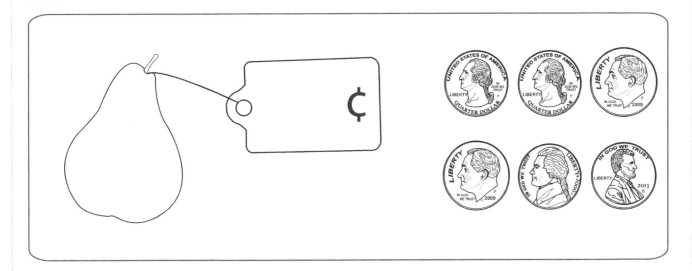

MONEY

Count the coins. Write the price of each cupcake.
Color the cupcakes.

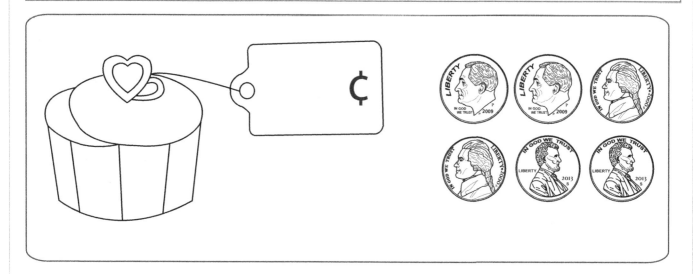

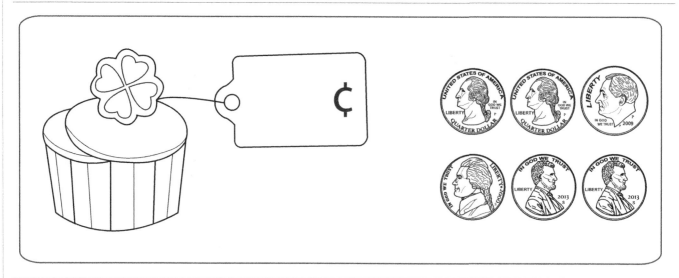

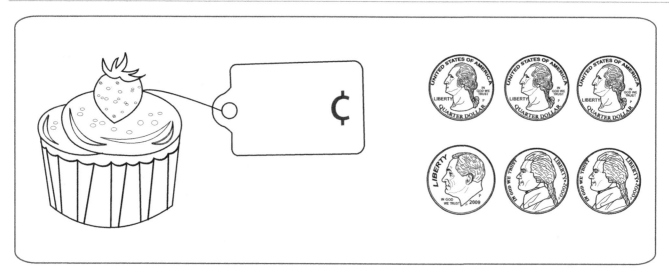

Kindergarten Math

Completed ✓

CONGRATULATIONS!
You are
AWESOME!

Recommended next skills

ISBN: 1777421152

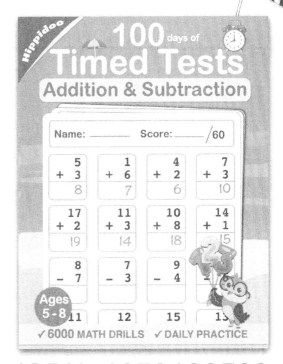

ISBN: 1679103709

Get it Today

Psst! Parents/Teachers,

Don't forget to claim your FREE eBook if you haven't done so already. It's an incredible resource for your child's math journey. Take advantage now!

To get this free ebook, email me at
sujatha.lalgudi@gmail.com

Title the email "KG Math" to get your copy of the free Math eBook!

Thank you
Sujatha Lalgudi

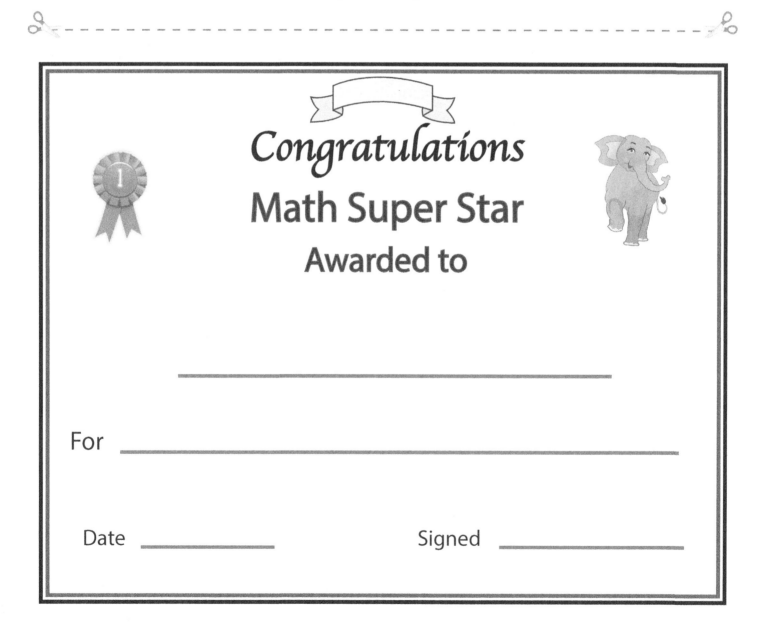

Congratulations
Math Super Star
Awarded to

_____

For _____

Date _____   Signed _____

Made in the USA
Monee, IL
28 August 2023

41356920R00063